WORKBOOK

For

me and white supremacy

Combat racism,
Change the world, and
Become a good ancestor

LAYLA F. SAAD

Roger Press

ISBN: 978-1-952663-28-4
Copyright © 2020 by: Roger Press

All rights reserved. This book or any portion thereof may not be reproduced or used in any manner whatsoever without the express written permission of the publisher except for the use of brief quotations in a book review.

Table of Contents

ABOUT THE AUTHOR 4
PART 1 5
INTRODUCTION 5
WHAT IS WHITE SUPREMACY? 5
PART 2: THE WORK 13
DAY 1: YOU AND WHITE PRIVILEGE 13
DAY 2: YOU AND WHITE FRAGILITY 18
DAY 3: YOU AND TONE POLICING 22
DAY 4: YOU AND WHITE SILENCE 26
DAY 5: YOU AND WHITE SUPERIORITY 29
DAY 6: YOU AND WHITE EXCEPTIONALISM 33
DAY 7: WEEK 1 REVIEW 36
WEEK 2: ANTI-BLACKNESS, RACIAL STEREOTYPES, AND 37
CULTURAL APPROPRIATION 37
DAY 8: YOU AND COLOR BLINDNESS 37
DAY 9: YOU AND ANTI-BLACKNESS AGAINST BLACK WOMEN 41
DAY 10: YOU AND ANTI-BLACKNESS AGAINST BLACK MEN 45
DAY 11: YOU AND ANTI-BLACKNESS AGAINST BLACK CHILDREN 48
DAY 12: YOU AND RACIST STEREOTYPES 51
DAY 13: YOU AND CULTURAL APPROPRIATION 54
DAY 14: WEEK 2 REVIEW 57
WEEK 3: ALLYSHIP 58
DAY 15: YOU AND WHITE APATHY 58
DAY 16: YOU AND WHITE CENTERING 61
DAY 17: YOU AND TOKENISM 63
DAY 18: YOU AND WHITE SAVIORISM 67
DAY 19: YOU AND OPTICAL ALLYSHIP 70
DAY 20: YOU AND BEING CALLED OUT/CALLED IN 73
DAY 21: WEEK 3 REVIEW 77
WEEK 4: POWER, RELATIONSHIPS, AND COMMITMENTS 77
DAY 22: YOU AND WHITE FEMINISM 77
DAY 23: YOU AND WHITE LEADERS 81
DAY 24: YOU AND YOUR FRIENDS 84
DAY 25: YOU AND YOUR FAMILY 86
DAY 26: YOU AND YOUR VALUES 89
DAY 27: YOU AND LOSING PRIVILEGE 91
DAY 28: YOU AND YOUR COMMITMENTS (CONCLUSION) 94

ABOUT THE AUTHOR

LAYLA F. SAAD, a female speaker, writer, and podcast host on leadership, identity, race, social change, and personal transformation. Layla F. Saad is a Black, East African, British, Arab Muslim born and bred in the West but lives in the Middle East. Layla has always been an individual of unique personality with an intersection of identities where she can draw opulent and captivating perspectives. Layla's work is compelled by her obsession with being a good ancestor and leave behind a legacy of freedom and healing for posterity.

Layla's first book – "Me and White Supremacy" was formerly digital which turned out to be a bestseller that got more than one hundred thousand people worldwide before it became a book. She studied law at Lancaster University in the United Kingdom and graduated with a Bachelor of Law. She is married to Sam, blessed with two children, Maya and Mohamed, and lives in Doha, Qatar. Layla's work has positively affected educational institutions, homes, and the workplace all over the world that seek personal and collective change.

PART 1
INTRODUCTION
WELCOME TO THE WORK

This is a twenty-eight-day guide to help you explore and get rid of your relationship with white supremacy. This is an anti-racism tool that can help individuals with white privilege comprehend and own their contribution to the oppressive system of white supremacy.

It helps individuals be responsible for undoing the way the system displays within themselves and their communities. The idea of this book is to nurture individuals with the desire to become a good ancestor. This can only be possible by creating change and healing internally/externally to prepare the path for those behind to walk through. This desire is so that the world is left in a better place than we found it.

White supremacy wasn't created by those who are alive now, but it is propagated by the respecters of "white privilege". The idea behind this book is to question, defy, and destroy this system that has hurt and killed a lot of black, Indigenous, and People of Color (BIPOC). This book is partly educational and motivational. This will expand your emotional, intellectual knowledge, understanding of racism, and white supremacy by looking at different multifaceted aspects of white supremacy and its operation. But more importantly, help you begin the feasible journey of ending racism (anti-blackness – a form of racism) which is still very much alive today. So be ready to work!

WHAT IS WHITE SUPREMACY?

White supremacy is an idea by a racist who believes that white people are superior more than other races and so they should be dominant in that regard as well. This twisted idea is passed on to one generation after another. Now, white dominance is not just an individual's perception; it is a structure upheld by an institution.

How does white supremacy look like on a personal level? Tackling the subject matter begins from individual inner work and will bring about effective changes since a lot of people belong to one system or institution or the other. The idea here is not to change how things look but changing the way things are, starting from inside out – the family, the business place, the community, and then to the world at large. White supremacy is not a term for bad people, neo-Nazis, and far-right extremists alone. It is very wrong and dangerous as it empowers the notion that white supremacy is an ideology only upheld by a small fraction of white people when it is the dominant group (a far larger group) of whites. Many whites feel the word "white supremacy" doesn't apply to them, that all men are equal and they don't treat people differently because of their skin tone – but that is not true.

White supremacy is a worldview, a paradigm, an ideology, an institutional system that one is born into because of white privilege. This is not talking about the physical color of your skin but the systemic institutionalizing, historic, present legislating, and societal conditioning of the structure of whiteness as intrinsically superior to people of other races. In the books, the oppressive racist system of operation has been abolished several years ago but these practices are still carried out on BIPOC. There is still subtle and overt discrimination, abuse, the killing of BIPOC in places dominated by whites, abuse, and many more to date. This is so because white supremacy is still the dominant paradigm by which the white society operates.

This is us looking deeper and finding out why white means better, more credible, superior, more deserving, more worthy, and more valuable, thereby leaving those not covered by the white privilege to suffer when we all are humans with blood flowing through our veins. But, its empire can crumble. White supremacy is what we are born into; its system has granted you unmerited privileges, power, and protection; but it, in turn, blinds your eye from seeing or stops to reason what happens to those who are not under the white privilege. Did you just feel guilt in your gut? Or was it anger, nausea, and frustration? Whichever you felt was as a result of the side of the divide you belong to. It's time to get up and challenge your involvement in this system and work at dismantling it from within and then the world.

Who is this work for?
This isn't only for the people of color but for everyone identified as white, bi-racially, multi-racially, white-passing, and anyone benefiting from white privilege under the white supremacy system. This will elicit various emotions like grief, shame, anxiety, confusion, anger, fear, and remorse. But don't beat yourself up about this, instead, use this as a tool to checkmate your participation within the system of privilege designed to benefit only the whites.

What you will need to do this work
There are three things you will need for this work;

1. Your truth
2. Your love
3. Your commitment

YOUR TRUTH

Only your truth can make this work for you. Tell your truth and leave absolutely nothing behind. It's the entirety of what you put in here that you will take out. Tell the truth no matter how ugly it looks or sounds, this will help to dig deep to the rotten core of your internal white supremacy and churn out something beyond transformational. If the tenets in this book are diligently observed then it can bring about some level of personal healing as well. But above all, this piece should heal and restore the dignity of BIPOC.

YOUR LOVE

Having a strong interest in this work is to love and believe in something bigger than your self-gain. It is the belief that every human deserves freedom, equality, and dignity that makes you embark on this fruitful journey. If love is the reason you began this journey; then I am hopeful it will make you persevere through it all.

YOUR COMMITMENT

This isn't an easy journey to embark on. White supremacy is a system that oppresses people who are not covered by white privilege; so it is evil. Bringing it to a halt will not be easy, besides it's been sitting in you for a long time, and exterminating it will take a conscious process of erasing. Remember, nothing good comes easy. Pinpoint an intentional reason for this commitment as this will help to keep your concentration and zeal burning so you can carry out your anti-oppression walk unaided and undiscouraged.

How to use this book
Tips to help you use this book as a self-guided journey;

1. Keep a journal close by for note-taking.
2. Maintain your own pace. Just because it is a 28-day challenge doesn't mean you lose the right to go at your own pace. It's no race but a journey.
3. Do not generalize. Don't generalize about the whites nor speak like you are no longer white or like you don't benefit from white privilege. It's not about the experiences, beliefs, and thoughts of others but yours.

If it's your first time, go through this workbook in a sequence you don't lose any thought as you go on. After that, go in intuitively after the twenty-eight days challenge completion. Or better still; go through it as it best pleases you or as it concerns your area of interest. You can either work on it alone or with a group of people with the same interest at heart. The idea is that you work.

Self-care, support, and sustainability
This is a very challenging job and the above will come in very handy. Many who have participated in this work have confessed that it affected and challenged them emotionally, physically, and spiritually. Enough self-care is needed as you get to root out your internalized white supremacy because it will greatly affect your spirit, body, and soul. Sustaining this work can only work if you invest in your self-care (not manicure or spa), meaning you stay grounded and connected to your body and emotions as well. In other not to be lonely; seek moral

support by reaching out to other people that share similar interest in your community or family and friends.

Emotions like anxiety, shame, apathy, anger, rage, grief, and confusion will come your way if you are neck-deep into this work. Don't shove these feelings; they are normal and an integral part of this process. Those feelings rehumanize you and mean you are about to wake up from your slumber. White supremacy is what has numbed you of the pain that racism brings, so this work is here to help you relive your truth and the pain associated with racism.

- **Lessons**
    1. White supremacy is a racist idea who believes that white people are superior more than other races and so they should be dominant in that regard as well.
    2. White supremacy is a sick idea passed on from one generation to another.
    3. White dominance is not just an individual's perception; it is now a structure upheld by an institution.
- **Issues surrounding the subject matter**
    1. What is white supremacy to you?

    _____
    _____
    _____
    _____

    2. Communicate how white supremacy has been demonstrated to you in your place of work, at the cafeteria, at school or where ever and how did you react to it?

_____
_____
_____
_____

3. How does white supremacy show up for you?

_____
_____
_____
_____
_____

- **Goals**
    1. Why do you think you react in the way you do as it concerns discussions on white supremacy?

    _____
    _____
    _____
    _____
    _____

    2. Write down all the thoughts and feelings that come to mind when the subject of white supremacy is mentioned.

    _____
    _____
    _____
    _____
    _____

- **Action steps**

1. Open up your heart to this in other to rid yourself of white supremacy and get more informed of ways you passively encourage racism.
- **Checklist**
    1. Let go of the belief of white supremacy, it needs to be annihilated from your system.

PART 2: THE WORK

These first 7 days of the challenge will consist of some of the basic foundations of white supremacy. Some of which are; white privilege, white fragility, white silence, and white exceptionalism. My advice, begin this journey with a beginner's mindset even if you are familiar with some of the terms been discussed here. Let's go on this cruise curious and eager.

DAY 1: You and White Privilege
DAY 2: You and White Fragility
DAY 3: You and Tone Policing
DAY 4: You and White Silence
DAY 5: You and White Superiority
DAY 6: You and White Exceptionalism
DAY 7: Week 1 Review

DAY 1: YOU AND WHITE PRIVILEGE

WHAT IS WHITE PRIVILEGE?

White privilege has been a systemic, legislative and cultural norm in existence for a very long time but Peggy McIntosh – a Women's studies scholar made it popular by her 1988 paper on "White Privilege and Male Privilege: A Personal Account of Coming to See Correspondences Through Work in Women's Studies." The paper displayed many examples of white privilege. She made the world understand that white privilege is likened to an invisible insubstantial package of special provisions, compass, assurances, visas, passports, tools, clothes, maps, emergency gears, codebooks, guides, and blank checks. They are the unmerited advantages granted to one identified as white. White privilege is useless in the absence of white supremacy. Science has made it clear that race is not a biological fact but a social concept.

Despite our variances in hair texture, skin color, and other physical traits, hereditarily, we are all largely the same. Nevertheless, as race is an intensely held social construct for the existence of white supremacy, we are not treated alike. White privilege seems to make a difference between you and another.

Haven said that about white privilege, there are still many people who go about saying white privilege is not real but its just a way to make the whites feel bad about themselves. How can that even be said, in a world where there is racial discrimination in employment, chattel slavery of African people, and racial segregation in schools? Does that even make any sense? The whites argue that they are the ones being oppressed and marginalized. They claim to have had those privileges in the past but it doesn't apply anymore in modern-day.

Due to the legal changes in civil rights, one will think that the extremely held construct of being biologically different in race and superiority of race will end. Well, it didn't help. From a very young age, children are been told and prepared whether the institution already laid down in the society will favor them or otherwise, based on them been white or people of color. Today, people of color are not rewarded for the same effort they put into work. They are made to struggle much more than necessary.

This shows at school, at work, and even on the street. White privilege sips into anything, it can bring about gender privilege, age privilege, class privilege, sexuality privilege, able-bodied privilege, and more.

SOME WAYS TO IDENTIFY WHITE PRIVILEGE;
1. My children do not need any form of education in other to be aware of systemic racism for them to be protected daily.
2. I can choose to be amongst people of my race if I want to.
3. Our national heritage or civilization was fought for people of my color.
4. Always being race-conscious and segregates on everything.
5. My race doesn't single me out when the IRS audits my tax returns or when a traffic cop pulls me over.
6. My legal and health insurance is covered because of my race.

WHY DO YOU NEED TO LOOK AT WHITE PRIVILEGE?

White privilege is the incentive received by the whites and white-passing people in exchange for contributing to the system of white supremacy—whether voluntary or involuntary.

For you to crumble white supremacy, you have to be able to identify it when you come in contact with one, understand how white privilege is a crucial part of your life, how being white benefits you, and what life is reduced to for people who lack your kind of privileges.

- **Lessons**
  1. White privilege is the incentive received by the whites and white-passing people in exchange for contributing to the system of white supremacy—whether voluntary or involuntary.
  2. White privilege is a systemic, legislative, and cultural norm in existence for a very long time.
- **Issues surrounding the subject matter**

1. Will you say you identify as a person with white privilege and why?

   _____
   _____
   _____
   _____
   _____

2. Based on your above response, were you ever told as a kid that your whiteness would work against you and that you will have to work harder to compensate your racial difference?

   _____
   _____
   _____
   _____
   _____

3. What is your definition of the true essence of white privilege?

   _____
   _____
   _____
   _____
   _____

- **Goals**
  1. What are the ways you hold white privilege? Reflect on your daily life and make a list of the various ways you hold white privilege in your individual life.

_____
_____
_____
_____
_____
_____
_____
_____
_____
_____

2. Recount the negative experiences your white privilege protected you from and the positive experiences your white privilege gave you that BIPOC does not have? This will help you to identify your white privileges.

_____
_____
_____
_____
_____

- **Action steps**
    1. Identify those aspects of your white privilege that makes you uncomfortable and start from there to question and get rid of them.
- **Checklist**
    1. Let go of the belief of white supremacy, it needs to be annihilated from your system.

DAY 2: YOU AND WHITE FRAGILITY
WHAT IS WHITE FRAGILITY?

White fragility is a phrase coined by author Robin DiAngelo. She defines white fragility as a state when the minutest amount of racial stress is intolerable triggering defensive moves.

White fragility has run deep into the white system. They get so sensitive and fragile when issues of race are been discussed that they elicit various emotions such as anger, confusion, defense, fear, etc. This is as a result of two things;

1. Non-exposure to conversations on racism (the blatant refusal to be adequately informed in that aspect).
2. Lack of understanding of what white supremacy is (they have a limited scope as to what racism means. They have no idea that it is marginalization, oppression, neglect, and discrimination at a systemic level).

HOW TO IDENTIFY WHITE FRAGILITY

1. Displaying emotions such as; anger, fear, defense, confrontation, shame, withdrawal, silence, crying, etc.
2. Calling the authorities on BIPOC when you feel uncomfortable about the subject of race.
3. Turning a blind eye to racial injustice on BIPOC.

WHY DO YOU NEED TO LOOK AT WHITE FRAGILITY?

Like the name implies, whites become very fragile in discussions about race. This ideology hinders one from having a smooth conversation about race without falling apart. Not being able to talk about racism and how you may have contributed your quota to make it stand; you will never be able to completely understand racism.

White fragility consists of the good/bad binary. The bad people are the racists while the good people and not racist.

The desire to be good can in turn prevent you from actually doing good. See yourself as part and parcel of the problem so you can be part of the solution as well. Try to listen to the BIPOC; don't switch to defense mode when the topic of race comes up. Show empathy and compassion, hear their pain, and discover what white privilege has shielded you from.

- **Lessons**
    1. White fragility is a state when the smallest amount of racial stress is intolerable triggering defensive moves.
    2. White fragility elicits emotions such as anger, confusion, defense, shame, withdrawal, silence, and fear.
    3. White fragility is a result of non-exposure to discussions on racism and a lack of understanding of what racism is.
- **Issues surrounding the subject matter**
    1. How does your white fragility show up in conversations about race? Do you freeze, fight, or take off, and why?

    _____
    _____
    _____
    _____
    _____

    2. How would you describe the feelings you feel when you hear the words "white people"? Does it make you uncomfortable and why?

    _____
    _____

_____
_____
_____

- **Goals**
    1. Recall your most vivid experience of white fragility. What conversation were you having? How old were you then? Where were you at the time? Why did it stir up white fragility from the inside of you? How did you feel during and after the conversation? And how do you feel about it today? This information will help you know the level at which your white fragility is and the lot you need to get rid of.

        _____
        _____
        _____
        _____
        _____
        _____
        _____
        _____
        _____

    2. How do you intend to stop using your fragility as a weapon against BIPOC by using reverse racism?

        _____
        _____
        _____

_____
_____
_____
_____
_____
_____
_____
_____
_____
_____
_____
_____
_____

- **Action steps**
    1. Find a way to extinguish fear and discomfort as a result of your white fragility that has hindered you from doing all you need to do concerning your antiracism work.
- **Checklist**
    1. Find out what triggers your white fragility and curtail it.

DAY 3: YOU AND TONE POLICING

WHAT IS TONE POLICING?

Tone policing is a scheme used by the individuals who enjoy the white privilege to mute those who don't by paying more attention to the tone of what is being said than the message itself. They claim that the tone was too angry and appraise the whites for their eloquence and soft tones when the subject of racism arises. This goes to say that the BIPOC is expected to look out for the white gaze (the supremacist lens) by which those with white privilege perceive BIPOC putting into consideration the comfort level of that individual's white fragility when speaking about racism.

Tone policing is considered racist so it is not spoken out loud. Those with white privilege often tone police BIPOC secretly and in their thoughts. It is in the abundance of the heart that shows what they will do physically if racism was something to be proud of. Tone policing has a lot to do with anti-blackness and racist stereotypes. Tone policing kills BIPOC's slowly and it exists anywhere white supremacy exists; in the school, on the internet, at home, educational institutions, at work, in spiritual spaces, and many more. This makes BIPOC's checkmate their tone before speaking in other not to come off angry as the white supremacist will term our voicing out to mean.

HOW TO RECOGNIZE TONE POLICING?

Tone policing is fully expressive in racial discussions thereby eliciting thoughts like:

1. I wish you will say what you are saying more graciously.

2. You have a very aggressive tone.
3. I refuse to listen to your pained experience of racism because you are too angry.
4. I feel ashamed by the language you are using to speak to me about your lived experience.
5. Appear more civilized and we will join your cause.
6. The language of your lived experience is hateful.
7. I can only listen to you when you are calm.
8. You are unproductive with the way you are going to speak about this issue.
9. Your lived experience you are speaking about is bringing in so much negativity into this place, focus on the positive.

Tone policing is mostly revealed during conversations on race and when BIPOC is accused of not complying with the white form of communication (using African American Vernacular English AAVE, speaking too loud)

WHY DO YOU NEED TO LOOK AT TONE POLICING?

Tone policing strengthens white supremacy. It keeps BIPOC in check and disempowers them. They feel when BIPOC is stripped of their credibility and attention then they will speak in the language that suits them. This reinforces the white supremacist ideology that whites know best and is ultimately superior.

- **Lessons**
  1. Tone policing is a scheme used by the individuals who enjoy the white privilege to mute those who don't by paying more attention to the tone of what is being said than the message itself.

2. Tone policing exists anywhere white supremacy exists.
- **Issues surrounding the subject matter**
    1. Have you ever used tone policing to silence or dismiss BIPOC? What kind of words can you use to describe what tone a BIPOC should adopt?

    _____
    _____
    _____
    _____
    _____

    2. What kind of tone policing thoughts have you concealed inside whenever you hear BIPOC talk about race or their lived experiences, even without saying it out loud?

    _____
    _____
    _____
    _____
    _____

- **Goals**
    1. As a BIPOC how do you intend to stop tone policing yourself and fully express how you feel about racism?

    _____
    _____
    _____
    _____
    _____

2. How do you intend to start paying more attention to the message than the tone being used?

_____
_____
_____
_____
_____

- **Action steps**
  1. Stop discounting BIPOC's real pain over racism just because it doesn't just fit with your world view of how people ought to talk.
- **Checklist**
  1. BIPOC, don't lose hope, this is all in a bid to sow seeds of doubt in your hearts and question the memory of your history. Don't let white supremacy purge you of what you have; our history is all we have left.

DAY 4: YOU AND WHITE SILENCE
WHAT IS WHITE SILENCE?
Just as the words above imply; it is when those with white privilege stay silent in issues of race and white supremacy arise.

A typical reason for this silence is white fragility; the fear of not falling apart when discussing race. Though that is not the only reason for this silence, the silence of good people is most disheartening. Today many people have lost their friendship as a result of race and the others who are still standing are because they are yet to talk about racism.

HOW TO IDENTIFY WHITE SILENCE?
Here are a few examples:
1. Staying silent when your colleagues of color are discriminated at work.
2. Staying silent/ leaving the room/changing the subject when family and friends make racist comments.
3. Staying silent in conversations about race because of your white fragility.
4. Staying silent and refusing to attend protest marches against racism.
5. Staying silent when a person of color is been mistreated and beaten especially in the presence of only white folks.

WHY DO YOU NEED TO LOOK AT WHITE SILENCE?
Many may think that white silence is harmless, some might go with the notion "I didn't do or say anything, I am neutral". Silence, in this case, is consent, you not doing anything to make the situation better is the same as perpetuating the evil. All of this boils down to white

supremacy. White silence is violence in itself. This happens every day of our lives in every sphere of society and it needs to stop.

- **Lessons**
    1. White silence is when those with white privilege stay silent when issues of race and white supremacy arise.
    2. White silence is violence.
    3. White silence may seem harmless but it is malignant.
- **Issues surrounding the subject matter**
    1. Explain the situations that elicit white silence from you?

    _____
    _____
    _____
    _____
    _____

    2. In what ways has your silence supported racist behavior?

    _____
    _____
    _____
    _____
    _____

    3. How are you benefiting from white silence?

    _____
    _____
    _____
    _____
    _____

- **Goals**

1. In what ways have you stayed silent in issues that border on race and racism?

   _____
   _____
   _____
   _____
   _____

2. In what ways will you begin to support the BIPOC movement and stop displaying white silence?

   _____
   _____
   _____
   _____
   _____

- **Action steps**
  1. Start to intentionally speak out for BIPOC, silence isn't golden in this case, it is evil.
- **Checklist**
  1. Silence is consent, before you think of turning a blind eye again; think of the generations of people you would have helped.

DAY 5: YOU AND WHITE SUPERIORITY
WHAT IS WHITE SUPERIORITY?

Superior as defined by Merriam-Webster means something of higher rank, importance, and quality. White superiority is drawn from the white supremacy belief that the whites or people of white-passing skin are better than and automatically deserves to dominate over people of color. This brought about the ideology behind the rightwing nationalism, neo-Nazis, and the KKK.

This is fully expressive in the doll test conducted by African American psychologists Drs. Kenneth and Mamie Clark to study the psychological effects of segregation on African American children. This test was conducted on African American children between the ages of three to seven. They were presented with four dolls that had similar features but differentiated by their skin tone – so two had white skin and the other two were black. These children were asked to pick the doll they preferred, identify their race, and why they preferred the one they chose. The result of the test showed that prejudice; segregation and discrimination have created a feeling of inferiority in the African American children which has damaged their self-esteem because most of the children desired the white doll and attributed more positive traits to it. All of this boils down to white supremacy that birth white superiority. More recently, a similar test like the kind stated above was conducted but mixed with white and black kids with results similar to the aforementioned. It had a lot of negatives ascribed to the dark skin and positive attributes to the dark skin.

HERE ARE DISPLAYED WHITE SUPERIORITY

1. Tone policing
2. Choosing and uplifting the European standards of beauty (lighter skin tone, rosy cheeks, straight hair, and pink lips) over kinky-haired and dark-skin women seen in the TV and the media.
3. Accepting the widely accepted way the white people speak and regard the African American Vernacular English (AAVE) as "ghetto".
4. Choosing to read books only by white authors.
5. Working predominantly with white service providers.
6. Primarily showing support for white leaders; be it political or nonpolitical.
7. Residing in the white part of town.
8. Expecting that BIPOC would serve you by providing free emotive labor around racialism.
9. Believing whether overtly or covertly to be smarter, wiser, more valuable, more sophisticated, more spiritual, more beautiful, more refined, etc.
10. Only sharing the works of BIPOC that supposedly doesn't offend other white people.

WHY DO YOU NEED TO LOOK AT WHITE SUPERIORITY?

White superiority is the foundation of white supremacy. This belief is not always a conscious one. It is even mostly hidden and rarely spoken about but it exists in our society and practiced daily.

- **Lessons**
    1. White superiority is the foundation of white supremacy.
    2. White superiority is drawn from the white supremacy belief that the whites of people of white-passing skin are better than and automatically deserves to dominate over people of color.
- **Issues surrounding the subject matter**
    1. In what ways have you deliberately or subconsciously believe that you are better than BIPOC?

    _____
    _____
    _____
    _____
    _____

- **Goals**
    1. In what ways do you think you can become a better ancestor by ending white superiority?

    _____
    _____
    _____
    _____
    _____

- **Action steps**
    1. Identify all the ways you display white superiority and make plans to end it.
- **Checklist**

1. I don't know in what ways you may have displayed white superiority but don't hide from this. This is the root of white supremacy. Own it.

DAY 6: YOU AND WHITE EXCEPTIONALISM

WHAT IS WHITE EXCEPTIONALISM?

White exceptionalism is when an individual of white privilege exempts himself/herself from the benefits, effects, and conditions of white supremacy saying that antiracism does not apply to you.

White exceptionalism is seemingly a double-sided weapon that protects the whites and attacks the people of color. They are the ones with the opinion that racism is a black or brown thing and has got nothing to do with the whites. Whereas it is the whites that carry white exceptionalism like a badge of honor.

SOME EXAMPLES OF WHITE EXCEPTIONALISM DISPLAYED?

1. White exceptionalism shows up every time you see one of the issues surrounding the subject matter and think, I don't do that!
2. White exceptionalism is the conviction that you don't need to do any work and that you are doing your very best.
3. White exceptionalism is that silly voice in your head telling you can read this book but don't raise a finger to do any work.
4. White exceptionalism is the idea that makes you feel exceptionally special.

WHY DO YOU NEED TO LOOK AT WHITE EXCEPTIONALISM?

White exceptionalism is common in liberal, progressive, spiritual white people with a belief system that being these things exempts them or that they are above it all but "You are not"! And the belief that you are, makes you dangerous to BIPOC as you cannot see your connivance and you will not listen when it is being mirrored back to you.

- **Lessons**
    1. White exceptionalism is when an individual of white privilege exempts himself/herself from the benefits, effects, and conditions of white supremacy and exempts themselves from antiracism.
- **Issues surrounding the subject matter**
    1. What are the ways you have believed you are exceptional, either "one of the good ones or beyond the taming of white supremacy"?

    _____
    _____
    _____
    _____
    _____

    2. As a parent, how are you teaching your children white exceptionalism?

    _____
    _____
    _____
    _____
    _____
    _____
    _____
    _____
    _____

- **Goals**
  1. How do you intend to stop acting out of white exceptionalism when confronted with racial discussions with BIPOC?

     _____
     _____
     _____
     _____
     _____

  2. Recall explicitly how your childhood, the society (schools, parents, the media) teach you white exceptionalism and retrace your steps on ways you will impact the upcoming generation with the correct information about race?

     _____
     _____
     _____
     _____
     _____

- **Action steps**
  1. Search out ways your white exceptionalism has hindered you from showing up in allyship to BIPOC.
- **Checklist**
  1. White exceptionalism is seemingly a double-sided weapon that protects the whites and attacks the people of color.

DAY 7: WEEK 1 REVIEW

This is not a day off, BIPOC's don't receive a day's break off white supremacy. This is a time to reflect on everything you have read so far. Sit back and take inventory of what you have learned these six days, integrate, and move on. Be guided, the aim of this piece is not to root out shame but to draw up your truth, see it, own it, and figure out what you are going to do with it.

WEEK 2: ANTI-BLACKNESS, RACIAL STEREOTYPES, AND CULTURAL APPROPRIATION

It doesn't get any milder, prepare because the remaining parts of this workbook isn't to pat you on the back, this warning goes out most especially to the biracial and white-passing people of color/multicultural. You will likely feel like the oppressed and the oppressor at the same time.

As it gets tough, try not to evade the complicated questions and be sincere with your responses. Also, try not to do this alone. Share your thoughts with people of like minds.

DAY 8: You and Color Blindness
DAY 9: You and Anti-Blackness against Black Women
DAY 10: You and Anti-Blackness against Black Men
DAY 11: You and Anti-Blackness against Black Children
DAY 12: You and Racist Stereotypes
DAY 13: You and Cultural Appropriation
DAY 14: Week 2 Review

DAY 8: YOU AND COLOR BLINDNESS

WHAT IS COLOR BLINDNESS?

The color blindness spoken of in this case is race-based. This is when you don't see skin color and do not notice a disparity in race. And even if you do, you do not treat others differently nor do you oppress them based on their skin tone. The whites say it is rude for their children to call out the skin color of a black person. But their skin is dark so why reprimand a child for saying what he saw? This is because their parents have attributed the word black as synonymous to bad.

There are socially constructed terms of race, its either Black or white. Whites are even of the opinion that speaking different races is so acrimonious – it creates racism. There lays the big lie that posits that if we can only stop seeing race; then racism will go away. This sort of thinking is naïve but also very lethal. This is what Professor Eduardo Bonilla-Silva called "the new racism" in his book Racism without Racists: Color-Blind Racism and the Persistence of Racial Inequality in Contemporary America. Only a few whites claim to be racist while many others claim to be racially progressive. If that is the case, why is racism still on the rise? Why is BIPOC still oppressed? Color blindness is a predominantly deceptive way for people with white privilege to pretend that their privilege is fictitious.

COMMON STATEMENTS TO HELP IDENTIFY COLOR BLINDNESS

1. I do not see color, only people.
2. I don't see you as black.
3. "He or she is a person of color" – because saying black is found to be offensive.
4. Denouncing a black person's lived experience and saying something similar happened to him/her as a white person – meaning that didn't occur because he/she is black.
5. Speaking about races encourages racial division.

WHY DO YOU NEED TO LOOK AT COLOR BLINDNESS?

This is necessary because color blindness is harmful at many levels. It is an act of minimization and expurgation. It needs to be addressed immediately in other to stop the erasing of the impact of the black skin, the hair pattern, the accent, the languages, culture, spiritual traditions that qualifies one as a bonafide BIPOC just because they exist within white supremacy.

- **Lessons**
    1. Racial color blindness is when you don't see skin color and do not notice a disparity in race.
    2. Racial color blindness's true aim is to expunge BIPOC and make them nonexistent and inconsequential in society.
- **Issues surrounding the subject matter**
    1. Why do you think children are taught not to see colors?

    _____
    _____
    _____
    _____
    _____

    2. What is your opinion on "when we stop seeing race, then racism will go away"?

    _____
    _____
    _____
    _____
    _____

    3. List out all you have experienced about color-blindness. Whether you were the perpetrator of the harm or the one harmed?

    _____
    _____
    _____
    _____
    _____

4. What first comes to mind when you hear the word "white people" or when you have to say "black people"?

_____
_____
_____
_____
_____

- **Goals**
    1. What measures do you have laid down to help you debunk all you have been taught about color blindness and seeing color while growing up?

    _____
    _____
    _____
    _____
    _____
    _____
    _____
    _____
    _____

- **Action steps**
    1. What feeling do you have when BIPOC talk about race?
- **Checklist**
    1. Refusing to look at color is the same as refusing to look at you as a human with white privilege.

DAY 9: YOU AND ANTI-BLACKNESS AGAINST BLACK WOMEN
WHAT IS ANTI-BLACKNESS AGAINST BLACK WOMEN?

Malcolm X expressly called Black women the most neglected, disrespected, and unprotected people in America. I am sure that same applies outside America as well. Even the Award-winning actress Viola Davis spoke about the dearth of symbolism and the categorizing of Black women in movies. It doesn't end in the movie industry; similar treatment is evident in any other industry and community space.

Black women elicit several feelings in Individuals who enjoy white privilege and the whites such as fear, scorn, anger, pity, desire, confusion, awe, superiority, distrust, jealousy, and more. They perceive the black woman to either be super-humanized or dehumanized. It's either she is a queen/ the strong fearless black woman or she is unworthy of love, care, and attention as given to a typical white woman. Political commentator, professor, and author Melissa V. Harris-Perry pointed out in her book – Sister Citizen: Shame, Stereotypes, and Black Women in America. The main stereotypes ascribed to the black woman include; Jezebel, Strong Black Woman, Mammy, and Sapphire. These stereotyped names were born out of bias and violent North American history. Now, this experience is the same in other countries as black women as seen as wild, aggressive, ugly, unintelligent, angry, and strong.

All of these limit the unique individuality and worth of the black woman thereby leading to abuse, maltreatment, and even death. In short, the black woman has been dehumanized and marginalized to a very far extent. Nevertheless, no situation is unredeemable.

HOW DOES ANTI-BLACKNESS AGAINST BLACK WOMEN SHOW UP?

1. The depreciating, deprecating, and one-sided stereotyping of black women.
2. The false representation of black women in leadership roles in industries and community space.
3. The contempt and disrespect towards Black women's style and beauty.
4. The expectancy from white women that black women are to choose their gender over their race in feminist movements. They forget that these women are both black and women at the same time.
5. Having black female friends and business partners just to be seen as non-racist.
6. The strong desire for praise, approval, comfort, recognition, and acknowledgment from Black women so that you good about yourself on your antiracism quest.
7. Fetishizing the strength, culture, and beauty of a Black woman.

WHY DO YOU NEED TO LOOK AT ANTIBLACKNESS AGAINST BLACK WOMEN?

Black women's empowerment poses as a big threat to white supremacy. With this knowledge in hand, white supremacy will stop at nothing to hinder, demonize, stifle, harm, marginalize, and undermine Black women.

Knowing this, white supremacy works particularly endlessly hard to stifle, undermine, marginalize, demonize, and harm Black women.

- **Lessons**
    1. Black women are the most neglected, disrespected, and unprotected people in America and other parts of the world.
    2. Anti-blackness is born out of fear, confusion, awe, superiority, distrust, jealousy, and more.
- **Issues surrounding the subject matter**
    1. What are some of the general racial stereotypes dating back in history and in modern times —pronounced and unexpressed associated with Black women?

        _____
        _____
        _____
        _____
        _____

    2. Mention some of the stereotypes you have thought and negative suppositions you have concluded in your heart about Black women, and how have these affected in what manner you have treated them?

        _____
        _____
        _____
        _____
        _____
        _____

- **Goals**
    1. How do you think antiblackness can be excavated, challenged, and owned to enable the smooth practice of antiracism?

       _____
       _____
       _____
       _____
       _____

    2. What kind of relationship have you had and do you have with Black women, and how can you ensure that you are not friends with them just to prove to be a non-racist?

       _____
       _____
       _____
       _____
       _____
       _____
       _____
       _____

- **Action steps**
    1. Write down the ways you intend to start treating Black women the same as your fellow white women.
- **Checklist**
    1. If you have tone policed, projected white fragility, and white superiority on Black women, then you are racist.

DAY 10: YOU AND ANTI-BLACKNESS AGAINST BLACK MEN
WHAT IS ANTI-BLACKNESS AGAINST BLACK MEN?

Black men are time and again imprisoned in a one-dimensional visualizing of who and what they ought to be. This is quite obvious in the US where these Black men are stripped of their humanity to date. The whites still visualize Black men as unintelligent, stupid, and sexually aggressive towards white women. This was fully expressed in the heartbreaking tragedy of the 1989 Central Part Five that was wrongly accused and served six to thirteen years in prison for sexual assault crimes they didn't commit. When the Black man isn't feared; then his sexuality is fetishized. Many other whites see the Black man as a means to an end – making of biracial babies in other to feel black. The Black man is also given a stagnant stereotype of servitude just the same as the Black woman.

EXAMPLES OF DISPLAYED ANTI-BLACKNESS AGAINST BLACK MEN;

1. Labeling Black men as violent, lazy, less intelligent, criminal, and sexually aggressive.
2. Showing awe when a Black man's personality doesn't fit in the white supremacist stereotypes.
3. Be intimate with Black men to shock white family members.
4. Ascribing a Black man's success to drug dealing, entertainment, or being athletes.
5. Desiring approval from Black men to be considered "woke".

WHY DO YOU NEED TO LOOK AT ANTIBLACKNESS AGAINST BLACK MEN?

It is imperative because it is dehumanizing and upholds the imperialist white supremacist view of Black men as unintelligent, violent savages, and thugs who threaten the white race. This sort of stereotype is limiting and degrading.

- **Lessons**
    1. The whites still visualize Black men as unintelligent, stupid, and sexually aggressive towards white women.
    2. Black men are time and again imprisoned in a one-dimensional visualizing of who and what they ought to be.
- **Issues surrounding the subject matter**
    1. In what ways have you fetishized Black men?

    _____
    _____
    _____
    _____
    _____

    2. In what ways have you minimized, excluded, used, discounted, tone policed, or projected your white fragility and white superiority on Black men?

    _____
    _____
    _____
    _____
    _____

    3. What kind of stereotypes have you thought and adverse assumptions have you made about Black men that have made you treat them badly?

    _____
    _____

_____
_____
_____

- **Goals**
    1. What kind of relationship have you had and do you have with Black men, and how can you ensure that you are not friends with them or married to prove to be non-racist?

    _____
    _____
    _____
    _____

    2. How much liberty do you give Black men in your mind to be intricate and multidimensional human beings?

    _____
    _____
    _____
    _____
    _____

- **Action steps**
    1. Check inward today and get to the core of it in other to stop ensnaring Black men in a white supremacist story you made up yourself.
- **Checklist**
    1. Disregard what anyone says; you have the right to be whatever you want, wherever you want.

DAY 11: YOU AND ANTI-BLACKNESS AGAINST BLACK CHILDREN

WHAT IS ANTI-BLACKNESS AGAINST BLACK CHILDREN?

The image whites have of Black children is that they start as cute brown skin kids and then as they grow older they metamorphose into hoodlums. Society treats black children as less intelligent, non-civilized, and less worthy of achievement and success than everybody else. This limits the Black child and makes them feel inferior. Two latest U.S. studies reveal how Black children experience "adultification" – the experience of being seen and treated older than they are. Another study called "The Essence of Innocence" by Professor Philip Goff and his colleagues also revealed that Black boys are seen older than they truly are and also less innocent than their white counterparts. Thus the take that police violence on a Black boy is justified but not the same for children in the same age bracket.

In 2017, a revolutionary U.S. study titled "Girlhood Interrupted: The Erasure of Black Girls' Childhood" was issued by the Georgetown Law Center on Poverty and Inequality. The result of this study was the same as that of the Black boy stated above. More explicitly, it reveals Black girls need less; -nurturing, protection, support, and comfort. Black girls are believed to more independent, know more about adult topics, and know more about sex.

EXAMPLES OF DISPLAYED ANTI-BLACKNESS AGAINST BLACK CHILDREN

1. Unnecessary pity for black children.
2. Unnatural desire to birth or adopt Black children.
3. Wanting to save Black children.
4. Employing Black children as props in whatever medium.

5. The high expectancy of Black children to be far stronger than whites.
6. Adultification of Black children.
7. Being overly nice to Black children to prove to be nonracist.

WHY DO YOU NEED TO LOOK AT ANTIBLACKNESS AGAINST BLACK CHILDREN?

Anti-Blackness needs to be tackled at the early stage because that's where it begins. Black children are treated inferior and worthy of every ounce of racism meted out to them.

- **Lessons**
    1. Anti-blackness against Black Children is just another way for white people to affirm their children as good and that of the Black's as bad.
- **Issues surrounding the subject matter**
    1. How guilty are you with the examples displayed above of anti-blackness against black children?

    _____
    _____
    _____
    _____
    _____
    _____
    _____
    _____
    _____
    _____

- **Goals**

1. In what ways have you encouraged national racial stereotypes in time past and in recent times against Black children?

   _____
   _____
   _____
   _____
   _____

2. As a white or biracial parent of Black children, what are the antiracism work you have been doing on yourself and in your immediate community to make the world a safe space for your children and others around you?

   _____
   _____
   _____
   _____
   _____
   _____
   _____
   _____

- **Action steps**
    1. Eliminating anti-blackness can only be successful if it is rooted out from the very core. Start at the beginning.
- **Checklist**
    1. Black children are not exempted from the anti-blackness.

DAY 12: YOU AND RACIST STEREOTYPES

WHAT ARE RACIST STEREOTYPES?

White supremacy has not only affected Black people but every Indigenous people and People of Color (POC) all around the world. There exist damaging racist stereotypes about Black people and people of color. Overtime racist stereotypes have been enforced in the media and the collective subconscious of people to make sure they remain ridiculed, criminalized, marginalized, feared, and dehumanized. White supremacy is against anyone that isn't like them, and then they are therefore threats.

Racism and prejudice are not the same. Racism is the linking of prejudice with power, where the main racial group (those who are enjoying national privilege) dominates other racial groups and adversely affects other race at all levels. So, a BIPOC can hold prejudice against whites but cannot be racist concerning them. This is because they don't have the power over the oppressive system to turn that prejudice into domination in ways that white persons would be able to if the tables were turned.

Here are some of the broad groups: Asian people, Latinx people, Indigenous people, Arab people, Biracial, and multiracial people.

EXAMPLES OF RACIST STEREOTYPE WORDS...although differs based on the racial group and gender;- Poor, lazy, less educated, less intelligent, exotic, spicy, spiritual, sexist, oppressed, terrorists, drug dealers, domineering, effeminate, aggressive, demure, alcoholics, overachieving, helpless, and opportunists.

WHY DO YOU NEED TO LOOK AT RACIST STEREOTYPES?

This is necessary because racist stereotypes keep reinforcing the notion that people who are not covered by white privilege shouldn't be offered privilege because they are inferior, and a threat to white civilization.

- **Lessons**
    1. Darker-skinned people frequently experience more racism than lighter-skinned individuals.
    2. Racial groups experience more religious prejudice and discrimination related to certain racial groups.
    3. White supremacy aims to collapse all racial "others" into a group in other to dominate and marginalize properly.
- **Issues surrounding the subject matter**
    1. How have you treated darker-skinned Indigenous people and POC differently from those who are lighter-skinned?

    _____
    _____
    _____
    _____
    _____
    _____

    2. What are the racist stereotypes, thoughts, and beliefs you have held and still hold about different racial groups of people?

    _____
    _____
    _____
    _____
    _____
    _____

- **Goals**
    1. Make a detailed list of the various racial groups of people in your country noting what you have learned about you and racist?

    _____
    _____
    _____
    _____
    _____
    _____
    _____
    _____

    2. Mention the ways you have super-humanized parts of the personalities of Indigenous people and POC while degrading other parts?

    _____
    _____
    _____
    _____

- **Action steps**
    1. How will you begin to treat Indigenous children and non-Black children of color the same as white children?
- **Checklist**
    1. Revealing your racist stereotypes will go far to help you see how you can actively give to white supremacy by being certain that white supremacy's lies about the inferiority of those who are termed the "other".

DAY 13: YOU AND CULTURAL APPROPRIATION
WHAT IS CULTURAL APPROPRIATION?

With white supremacy, there is always a hierarchical influence and privilege dynamic at play. At the top we have those with white privilege holding institutional and psychological superiority positions; while the bottom has those without white privilege holding institutional and psychological inferiority. The dynamic portrayed above joined with a violent force made slavery and colonization feasible.

In contemporary times, speaking about cultural appropriation can be tricky because we are all now more culturally interconnected with the aid of the internet, and advancements in travel and technology. Cultural appropriation is the seizure and misappropriation of another culture's values, objects, norms, motifs, rituals, symbols, artifacts, and cultural elements. Given this, individuals that share similar cultural beliefs can say that a thing is culturally appropriative while the other from the same group beliefs it to be cultural appreciation; thus making it hard to classify what is cultural appropriation. Cultural appropriation is the exploitation of other people's culture by a dominant culture. The dominance well mentioned has to do with the historic and modern relationships existing amongst both cultures. Still existing today is racial color blindness, anti-blackness, and racist stereotypes,

WAYS CULTURAL APPROPRIATION SHOWS UP; fashion, hair (African hairstyles), beauty (rounder hips & thighs, thicker lips, and darker/tanned looking skin), spirituality, wellness (traditional healing modalities), music, cultural events, cultural holidays and linguistic styles.

WHY DO YOU NEED TO LOOK AT CULTURAL APPROPRIATION?

This issue needs urgent addressing because its aim is sinister. The actual aim of cultural appropriation is to erase the less dominant culture in the picture out of existence.

- **Lessons**
  1. Cultural appropriation occurs between a dominant and a marginalized culture.
  2. Cultural appropriation is the exploitation of other people's culture by a dominant culture.
- **Issues surrounding the subject matter**
  1. What notion did you bring to this book from the onset (are you a good white person or an ally to BIPOC) and what are you now?

     _____
     _____
     _____
     _____
     _____

  2. Why have you come to learn about the dehumanizing ways BIPOC are treated?

     _____
     _____
     _____
     _____
     _____
     _____

3. Are you are multiracial, biracial, or a Person of Color with white privilege, what have you gained from this week and how can you find grounding and self-care for yourself after this weighty week?

   _____
   _____
   _____
   _____
   _____

4. How does white supremacy work through you?

   _____
   _____
   _____
   _____
   _____

- **Goals**

   1. What have you learned about you and anti-blackness that can be used as a positive tool to end racism in your immediate environment?

   _____
   _____
   _____
   _____
   _____
   _____
   _____
   _____

2. How are you thinking contrarily as it concerns your white privilege, white tone policing, white fragility, white silence, white exceptionalism, and white superiority now?

_____
_____
_____
_____
_____
_____
_____
_____
_____

- **Action steps**
    1. Begin to call out white people practicing culturally appropriating.
- **Checklist**
    1. It is racism, and it has to be wrestled with.

DAY 14: WEEK 2 REVIEW

This is a time to reflect on everything you have read and imbibed on the concept of Color Blindness, You and Anti-Blackness against Black Women, You and Anti-Blackness against Black Men, You and Anti-Blackness against Black Children, You and Racist Stereotypes and You and Cultural Appropriation. Turn all your goals to physical manifestations, it is possible and it starts with you.

WEEK 3: ALLYSHIP

The concept of "allyship" has to do with the thoughts, behaviors, and actions that go hand in hand with the above term. Allyship is an intentional act by a person of privilege to be actively consistent to unlearn and reassess the workings of solidarity with a downgraded group. Allyship is not an identity but a lifetime process of constructing relationships grounded on trust, accountability, and consistency with sidelined individuals.

DAY 15: You and White Apathy
DAY 16: You and White Centering
DAY 17: You and Tokenism
DAY 18: You and White Saviorism
DAY 19: You and Optical Allyship
DAY 20: You and Being Called Out/Called In
DAY 21: Week 3 Review

DAY 15: YOU AND WHITE APATHY

WHAT IS WHITE APATHY?

Apathy is an absence of feeling or emotion. It is being indifferent, unconcerned, passive, detached, insensitive, etc. White apathy is present to protect oneself from participating in the oppression called white supremacy. White apathy isn't neutral, unlike white silence. White apathy isn't aggressive, but its passivity is lethal. When white apathy affirms your pain and grief, it does absolutely nothing to alleviate it. It is a system of oppression that gives unmerited advantages and privileges to a group of people at the detriment of others. It encourages criminalization, discrimination, racist stereotypes, and abuse.

Some factors that contribute to white apathy are; white privilege, white fragility, white silence, white exceptionalism, anti-blackness, and racist stereotypes.

FEW EXAMPLES OF HOW WHITE APATHY SHOWS UP:

1. Being tried or displaying perfectionism when it comes to contributing to anti-racism practices.
2. Doing little or nothing about antiracism and not zeal to commit to the work.
3. Displaying white silence, inaction, and white exceptionalism for being attached to the notion that you are a good white person.
4. Being lackadaisical about doing the work and ignoring the fact that BIPOC is in dire need of liberty from this apathy.
5. Taking your antiracism education for levity and procrastinating the work that needs to be done. And many more examples...

WHY DO YOU NEED TO LOOK AT WHITE APATHY?

White apathy strongly supports white supremacy. White supremacy fears that BIPOC has what it takes to overthrow them and take over their jobs, homes, safety, and wealth; so they withhold their privileges and power.

- **Lessons**
    1. White apathy is choosing to stay in the comfort zone of white supremacy and the privileges that come with it.
    2. Standing against your white apathy is to turn your back on white supremacy.

- **Issues surrounding the subject matter**
  1. Have you noticed people in your community (family, friends, and colleagues) who hold white privilege being apathetic about racism?

     _____
     _____
     _____

  2. What are the factors that contribute to white apathy generally or your display of white apathy?

     _____
     _____
     _____
     _____
     _____

- **Goals**
  1. List out all the ways you have been apathetic about racism and how you would have done things differently?

     _____
     _____
     _____
     _____
     _____

- **Action steps**
  1. Pulling down the pillars of white apathy starts with speaking out and not practicing white silence.
- **Checklist**
  1. White apathy and white silence are not the same.

DAY 16: YOU AND WHITE CENTERING

WHAT IS WHITE CENTERING?

It is no longer news – the White supremacy has a problem with Black centralization. Whether it is a novel, a journal, a movie, and many other ways to centrally portray the back race, the whites get very uncomfortable. Anything centered on Blacks is considered low class, irrelevant, and less mainstream. It is a crime to center anything on blacks except it is centered on the whites; exactly what white supremacy propagates.

HOW WHITE CENTERING IS DISPLAYED: White feminism, white Saviorism, false presentation of historical events just to take out its true essence, the overrepresentation of individuals with white privilege in positions of leadership, tone policing, responding to "#BlackLivesMatter" with "AllLivesMatter" or "BlueLivesMatter" and the valuing of European standards of beauty over the standards of BIPOC.

WHY DO YOU NEED TO LOOK AT WHITE CENTERING?

White centering is strong bedrock for white supremacy. It is easy to identify the regular racist display but it is almost impossible to know which degrades and obliterates BIPOC through white centering.

- **Lessons**
  1. White supremacy seeks dominance and not equality.
  2. Anything centered on Blacks is considered low class, irrelevant, and less mainstream.
- **Issues surrounding the subject matter**
  1. In what ways have you centered yourself as an individual holding white privilege in nonwhite conversations?

_____
_____
_____
_____
_____

- **Goals**
    1. In your opinion, how does white centering affect BIPOC?

    _____
    _____
    _____
    _____
    _____

    2. In what ways have you judged BIPOC as not being able to measure up to the white-centered standard of living?

    _____
    _____
    _____
    _____
    _____

- **Action steps**
    1. Make plans to make your world view less white-centered.
- **Checklist**
    1. Only when whiteness is decentered then white supremacy loses its power.

DAY 17: YOU AND TOKENISM

WHAT IS TOKENISM?

Nowadays the student body in our international educational sectors gets diverse by the day but the leadership and teaching aren't. The teachers are heavily dominated by whites while there are sparingly people of color. There is a need for diversity not just for the children of color but for the white children as well. This will give them a complete frame and buildup of what everyone's race is about. It is not enough for the student body to be filled with diversity but makes not so much impact when the group of teachers are all whites; these are the people who instill knowledge in our children and diversity is highly required.

That been said, it is clear and most certain that unconscious racial bias and anti-blackness will be displayed by these white teachers as a white privilege doesn't disappear magically. Tokenism is the act of making symbolic efforts to do a certain thing, principally by employing an inconsequential number of people from lessened groups to give the appearance of racial or sexual equality within a workforce.

This is a tactic by many organizations to use tokenism to solve the challenge of underrepresentation in other to appear as an organization not practicing racism and this is very rampant today.

COMMON KINDS OF DISPLAYED TOKENISM

Four kinds of tokenism:

1. Brand Tokenism- using the cultural elements of a very few BIPOC to make a notion diversity but not enacting it or practicing antiracism.
2. Storytelling Tokenism- using BIPOC characters to visually represent the look of diversity or supplement the key white characters.
3. Emotional Labor Tokenism- when people with white privilege implore BIPOC to emotionally deal with anything relating to racism thereby reducing them to their race.
4. Relational Tokenism- this is when a person of white privilege makes use of their relationship with BIPOC as evidence that they are not racist.

WHY DO YOU NEED TO LOOK AT TOKENISM?

Tokenism is highly deceptive and dehumanizing as it takes away the humanity of BIPOC's. Everything tokenism stands for is sinister. This is because the idea is to use it against another BIPOC thereby weaponizing one against the other.

Without understanding what tokenism is and committing not to practice it, white supremacy continues to control the narrative about what equality and dignity for BIPOC look like.

- **Lessons**
    1. Tokenism is the act of making symbolic efforts to do a certain thing, principally by employing an inconsequential number of people from lessened groups to give the appearance of racial or sexual equality within a workforce.
    2. Tokenism is highly deceptive and dehumanizing because it takes away the humanity of BIPOC's.

- **Issues surrounding the subject matter**
    1. In what ways have you used your relationship with BIPOC to justify your racism?

    _____
    _____
    _____
    _____
    _____

    2. In what ways have you tokenized BIPOC to corroborate your words, actions, and thoughts are not racist?

    _____
    _____
    _____
    _____
    _____

- **Goals**
    1. In what ways have you decided not to contribute to tokenism?

    _____
    _____
    _____
    _____
    _____
    _____
    _____

2. List out the ways you have tokenized and weaponized one BIPOC against another BIPOC and how would you have done things much better?

_____
_____
_____
_____
_____
_____
_____
_____
_____
_____

- **Action steps**
    1. Stop staying silent when tokenism is being displayed.
- **Checklist**
    1. With the knowledge of what tokenism is; stop its practice even as white supremacy doesn't stop at the end at controlling the narrative about what equality and dignity for BIPOC should be like.

DAY 18: YOU AND WHITE SAVIORISM

WHAT IS WHITE SAVIORISM?

White Saviorism streams from white supremacy. It is the belief that people who hold white privilege, believe to be superior in all aspect and are obligated to "save" BIPOC from their hypothetical inferiority and helplessness. Teju Cole clearly described white Saviorism when the white missionaries volunteered to travel to countries in Africa, Latin America, and Asia to "rescue" BIPOC from their nation's poverty and underdevelopment. These countries are perceived as corrupt, poor, and underdeveloped. Their technological advancements, business leaders, activists, creatives, engineers, scientists, and general development are watered-down and are rarely showcased.

The whites have painted themselves as saviors and heroes that came to the rescue of inferiors by what they call the "white intervention". White Saviorism is displayed in movies and fictional stories like The Blind Side, The Last Samurai, Avatar, The Great Wall, and many more movies that showcase whites as a savior to BIPOC.

WAYS WHITE SAVIORISM SHOWS UP

1. Going on missionary and volunteerism trips to BIPOC countries with the mission to lead and not serve.
2. Taking on savior hero narratives in fictional stories and movies.
3. Strong urge to speak on behalf of BIPOC's need
4. The belief that BIPOC's are from a "shithole" filled with corruption, underdevelopment, and poverty.

WHY DO YOU NEED TO LOOK AT WHITE SAVIORISM?

White Saviorism needs to be addressed urgently because it is more malignant that deceptively benign. We need to correct the notion that without whites BIPOC is inferior to people who enjoy white privilege.

- **Lessons**
  1. White Saviorism is when an individual with white privilege speaks over or on behalf of BIPOC believing that they know a better presentation of what should be said.
- **Issues surrounding the subject matter**
  1. Make a list of the white savior chronicles you have noticed yourself buying into be it consciously or unconsciously?

  _____
  _____
  _____
  _____
  _____
  _____
  _____

  2. Why do you feel that BIPOC are helpless and require intervention and help from people that hold white privilege?

  _____
  _____
  _____
  _____
  _____

- **Goals**

1. In what ways have you displayed Saviorism or spoken on behalf of BIPOC because you feel you can better express what they feel than themselves and what would you do differently next time?

   _____
   _____
   _____
   _____
   _____
   _____
   _____
   _____
   _____

2. In what ways do you intend to change the white Saviorism you hold dear?

   _____
   _____
   _____
   _____
   _____

- **Action steps**
    1. Make intentional efforts to change all the white Saviorism stereotypes you have inside of you.
- **Checklist**
    1. White Saviorism is another form of colonialism.

DAY 19: YOU AND OPTICAL ALLYSHIP
WHAT IS OPTICAL ALLYSHIP?
Optical Allyship is also known as "eye-service/visual allyship." Latham Thomas, an author and initiator of Mama Glow, a premier maternity lifestyle brand, defined optical allyship as that – allyship that solitary serves at the superficial level to platform the "ally."

It is all about making shallow statements that don't penetrate the surface to go beneath which is not aimed at breaking from the oppressive powers that be. These statements don't carry any weight and are therefore baseless. Here those who hold white privilege do little or nothing to help those oppressed by race but instead apply tokenism, white centering, white Saviorism, and more to fabricate a visual illusion of allyship.

Signs to show if an act of allyship is sincere or optical:

1. Intentions behind the allyship act just so you are not referred to as a racist, receive a social recognition reward and praise
2. To create a false look of diversity but it ends on the surface level.
3. When the allyship act is spearheaded by a white privilege holder who doesn't listen, partners, or follows the BIPOC leadership they intend to help.
4. When the act of allyship is performed in their comfort zone.
5. The white privilege holder switches to white fragility when confronted with BIPOC.

WHY DO YOU NEED TO LOOK AT OPTICAL ALLYSHIP?

It is no longer news that optical allyship is as harmful as its fellows – tokenism and white Saviorism. Optical allyship focuses on the person with white privilege and not the BIPOC needing support. It's all in a bid to do little or nothing and then be praised, rewarded, recognized globally, and seen as nonracist. As long as it is deceptive, it needs to go!

- **Lessons**
    1. Optical Allyship is also known as "eye-service/visual allyship."
    2. True allyship takes the struggles of BIPOC as theirs, stand up for BIPOC even when scared, transfer their white privilege benefits to BIPOC, sincerely share in the pain of BIPOC and not take the spotlight off of them at any point of the conversation as they share their pained experience.

- **Issues surrounding the subject matter**
    1. In what ways have you practiced optical allyship in antiracist issues?

    _____
    _____
    _____
    _____

    2. Is your motivation for being a race ally dependent on what others think about you or how you are perceived?

    _____
    _____
    _____

_____
_____

- **Goals**

    1. How do you intend to make your act of allyship more substantive and less symbolic?
    _____
    _____
    _____
    _____

    2. How do you think you can be a true allyship to those without white privilege?
    _____
    _____
    _____
    _____

- **Action steps**

    1. Make notes of positive ways you want to begin to respond when called out for optical allyship.

- **Checklist**

    1. If you seek reward for your act of allyship then you are practicing "optical allyship."

DAY 20: YOU AND BEING CALLED OUT/CALLED IN
WHAT IS BEING CALLED OUT OR CALLED IN?
White fragility is what showcases when being called out or called in. Calling out or calling in is all in a bid to draw attention to one's despicable, problematic, and oppressive display just to correct that behavior and make amends.

"Calling-out" is a public display of reprimanding oppressive behavior while "Calling-in" is a private admonishing to the individual concerned just to address the behavior without making a public spectacle of the situation. There are lots of concerns and factors as regards the subject matter; Tone policing, power dynamics, expected respect from BIPOC, emotional labor involved for BIPOC, nature of the relationship existing between persons called out/in and the one calling out/in, the employed optical allyship and the venomousness that comes along with call-out culture as opposed to call-outs occasionally being the best and only approach available.

KINDS OF REACTIONS WHEN BEING CALLED OUT AND CALLED IN

Defensive, derailed, crying, withdrawal, silent, walking out, minimizing impact, tone policing, denying your racist action because you are racially color blind, tokenizing BIPOC to prove a point, listening less and talking more to the people calling you out/in and centering on ways to quickly get things fixed via optical allyship.

WHY DO YOU NEED TO LOOK AT BEING CALLED OUT AND CALLED IN?

Calling-out and calling-in people threaten people with white privilege who hide behind white supremacy to make them look good, virtuous, and morally right. It is this fear that deters genuine antiracism from being practiced. In your antiracism work, there is a thin line from being scared of not wanting to be called out/in which leads to perfectionism.

- **Lessons**
    1. "Calling-out" is a public display of reprimanding oppressive behavior while "Calling-in" is a private admonishing to the individual concerned just to address the behavior without making a public spectacle of the situation.
- **Issues surrounding the subject matter**
    1. In what ways have you focused on yourself and your intentions over BIPOC and the effect of your actions?

    _____
    _____
    _____
    _____
    _____

    2. What did you feel, think, say, or do when called out/in?

    _____
    _____
    _____
    _____
    _____

    3. What are your biggest fears of being called out/in?

    _____
    _____
    _____

_____
_____

- **Goals**
    1. When you happened to be called out/in, are you well-resourced sufficiently to answer in ways that will help you learn and do better, or will you give in to white fragility and crumble?

        _____
        _____
        _____
        _____
        _____

    2. In your antiracism work where does your biggest challenge lay?

        _____
        _____
        _____
        _____
        _____

    3. Write down all you have learned about yourself and your unique, personal brand of white supremacy?

        _____
        _____
        _____
        _____
        _____

- **Action steps**

1. Set aside your unconscious beliefs about your racial superiority and exceptionalism and give a listening ear to BIPOC with empathy.
- **Checklist**
    1. Fear is a strong deterrent to the practice of genuine antiracism.

DAY 21: WEEK 3 REVIEW

This week addressed behaviors associated with the practice of allyship and how white supremacy continues to be propagated in actions and behaviors that seem moral but reveals the racist status quo hiding underneath. The fact that antiracism and social change are yet to be collectively propagated is why white supremacy thrives to date. Keep working at pulling down the structures of white supremacy by engaging in racial conversations, lay down your white fragility and be prepared to listen to feedback and work your way to the top (liberty from white supremacy).

WEEK 4: POWER, RELATIONSHIPS, AND COMMITMENTS

This week focuses on your relationships with others who hold positions of white privilege, your values, and obligations to antiracism. This week, our focus is on the below not discounting all we have learned in the past weeks:

DAY 22: You and White Feminism
DAY 23: You and White Leaders
DAY 24: You and Your Friends
DAY 25: You and Your Family
DAY 26: You and Your Values
DAY 27: You and Losing Privilege
DAY 28: You and Your Commitments

DAY 22: YOU AND WHITE FEMINISM

WHAT IS WHITE FEMINISM?
The feminism referred to here can also pass for "mainstream" feminism. Feminism is relative to different people regardless of

gender identity or the nature of their relationship with feminism. What should resonate with us is how white feminism affects BIPOC.

Feminism refers to ideologies and movements – be it social and political with a common goal of establishing and achieving economic, political, and social equality of genders. Feminism focuses on the struggles of white women devoid of addressing divergent forms of domination faced by ethnic marginalized women and women lacking other privileges. White feminism requires BIPOC to put aside their race and challenges with racism and come together as sisters bound together by gender and sexism. They forget that as a white woman, they have nothing to be worried about their race since they have white privilege but BIPOC setting aside their race automatically means to act white. Also asking BIPOC to center on gender in place of race is to tell her to put her diverse identities in a hierarchical order. She is Black and woman, not; Black then woman.

EXAMPLES OF HOW WHITE FEMINISM SHOWS UP:

1. White feminists talking about the pay gap between men and women and leave behind the pay gap between white women and BIWOC (Black, Indigenous, Women of Color).
2. White feminist spirituality culturally seizes and wipeouts BIPOC spirituality.
3. White feminists attending white related marches but don't show up in related numbers for Black women marches (Black Lives Matter marches)
4. White feminist ignores or is ignorant of the U.S. Black maternal health crisis as it doesn't affect white women.

5. White feminism focuses on white women leaders but looks down and betrays BIWOC leaders.
6. White feminists disbelieving Muslim feminists because they wear hijabs.
7. White feminism disregards the revolutionary works of Black feminists like Angela Davis, Kimberlé Crenshaw, Alice Walker, Audre Lorde, Bell Hooks, and other BIWOC feminists.

WHY DO YOU NEED TO LOOK AT WHITE FEMINISM?

White feminism is an annex of white supremacy. Overtime white feminism hasn't lived up to what it is supposed to uphold. Instead, it aims to strip BIWOC of their originality and race.

- **Lessons**
  1. Feminism focuses on the struggles of white women devoid of addressing divergent forms of domination faced by ethnic marginalized women and women lacking other privileges.
- **Issues surrounding the subject matter**
  1. To what degree will you say your knowledge of feminism has been under the concern of gender only?

  _____
  _____
  _____
  _____
  _____

- **Goals**

1. How would you say your feminism has been white-centered?

   _____
   _____
   _____
   _____
   _____

2. In what ways has your feminism neglected or minimized the issues of BIPOC and how can you rewrite this wrong?

   _____
   _____
   _____
   _____
   _____

- **Action steps**
  1. Stop centering BIWOC's, what ways will you make this work?

     _____
     _____
     _____
     _____
     _____

- **Checklist**
  1. If your feminism rejects, discounts, or simply ignores BIPOC leaders then you have failed at feminism.

DAY 23: YOU AND WHITE LEADERS

YOU AND WHITE LEADERS

This part looks at you and white leaders, most especially individuals who hold positions of white privilege in places of power, leadership, and authority whom you come into contact with. Models of leaders include public figures, coaches, teachers, mentors, speakers, authors, management at your place of work or other institutions, community leaders, worship leaders, project leaders, politicians, and so on.

WHY DO YOU NEED TO LOOK AT YOUR RELATIONSHIP WITH WHITE LEADERS?

These white people of privilege who hold leadership positions have a huge responsibility to you and me. The white privileged leaders are weighty and influential. They can affect a greater impact on the way BIPOC is treated by enacting policies and practices to better the lives of the marginalized minority BIPOC.

We should continue to ignite our leaders to effect the changes we want to be seen and not keep quiet because they are yet to do anything about our cries and wails.

- **Lessons**
  1. White leaders are influential and hold high positions of authority.
- **Issues surrounding the subject matter**
  1. Does your fear of loss of privilege hinder you from requiring white leaders to do better?

- **Goals**
    1. With the knowledge you now have of white supremacist behaviors, how will you respond when you observe white leaders acting out tone policing, cultural appropriation, white Saviorism, optical allyship, claim color blindness, and enabling anti-Black tropes or racist stereotypes on BIPOC?

2. Are you in a leadership position, if yes, how do you intend to answer your conducts going forward and be more accountable?

_____
_____
_____
_____
_____
_____
_____
_____
_____

- **Action steps**
  1. Be more aware of your white leaders and how involved they are in antiracism work. Also imploring them to look beyond the optical effects of diversity.
- **Checklist**
  1. If we stay quiet, nothing will change.

DAY 24: YOU AND YOUR FRIENDS

YOU AND YOUR FRIENDS

Today's concentration doesn't end with your closest friends as that can pose as the safest comfort zone to a lot of people. Instead spread your tentacles out to all your circle of friends and acquaintances where ever they work in your community and outside that community and their given industries.

WHY DO YOU NEED TO LOOK AT YOUR RELATIONSHIPS WITH YOUR FRIENDS?

A true friend will have a positive influence on you and vice versa. Influence goes a long way and it's very vital in any relationship. Even though it is an unconscious act of antiracism carried out by your friend, it will travel far in the hearts of the person it is been administered to. Thus, you need to be careful what you display in the presence of your white friends, if it white silence/white apathy; they will return similar energy back to the world.

- **Lessons**
  1. Our friends carry a great influence that can affect our antiracism work.
- **Issues surrounding the subject matter**
  1. In what ways have you allowed your friends to influence you not to involve in antiracism work?

_____
_____
_____
_____

- **Goals**
  1. In what ways have you responded when you witness racist words and actions from friends in your life and how would you respond now knowing all you know now on race?

     _____
     _____
     _____
     _____
     _____

  2. Are there some people you feel extra comfortable speaking to than others? And why is that?

     _____
     _____
     _____
     _____
     _____

- **Action steps**
  1. It is your responsibility to address any display of white supremacy with your friends due to your influence on friendship.
- **Checklist**
  1. Your friendship is a valuable tool in the eradication of white supremacy from the very root.

DAY 25: YOU AND YOUR FAMILY

YOU AND YOUR FAMILY

Every family has its complexities that make them unique in some sort of way. Family is filled with secrets and scandals but that doesn't stop the work of eradicating white supremacy and antiracism to halt.

WHY DO YOU NEED TO LOOK AT YOUR RELATIONSHIP WITH YOUR FAMILY?

The family has a great deal of influence just as you have with your friends and acquaintances. The family is the origin where we learned or didn't learn about white supremacy and white privilege. Parents have more influence over their children, so the question is what have you instilled in your child as a parent propagating antiracism? On the other hand, there are many white homes with little or no knowledge of antiracism; it is the duty of the exposed one to deepen your family's orientation of antiracism and its practices.

- **Lessons**
  1. The family has a great deal of influence and is the origin where we learned or didn't learn about white supremacy and white privilege.
- **Issues surrounding the subject matter**
  1. Why do you place white comfort above antiracism in your family?

_____
_____
_____
_____

2. As a parent/caregiver, how do you speak to your children/wards about racism past "we don't see color" and how early in their lives did you speak to them about white privilege?

_____
_____
_____
_____
_____
_____
_____
_____
_____
_____
_____
_____
_____

- **Goals**
    1. Have you ever let perfectionism get in the way of ensuring racial conversations with your family, what will you do differently henceforth?

    _____
    _____
    _____
    _____

2. How do you intend to begin to have deeper conversations with your family about racism?

_____
_____
_____
_____
_____

- **Action steps**
    1. Be encouraged to participate and organize your family to come out for BIPOC in your communities from a standpoint of volunteering and not white Saviorism.
- **Checklist**
    1. Retrace and readdress the racist views that have you internalized from your family.

DAY 26: YOU AND YOUR VALUES

YOU AND YOUR VALUES

By now you will know that this work is a lifelong practice. These remaining parts are far more important because it is what will keep you grounded on your goals even after these twenty-eight days are completed. You and your values; our values serve as our rules, beliefs, standards, and principles that guide how we live life and it largely affects where we choose to place our energy.

WHY DO YOU NEED TO LOOK AT YOUR VALUES?

Holding white privilege and being conditioned by the very system that propagates it means you have some subliminal values that are white supremacist in nature. There may be clashes in your conscious and unconscious values leaving you battling whether to succumb to you white supremacy or join the antiracism work. If your values aren't grounded on strong stable grounds, then white supremacy and its other mean family members will shake the very ground your positive values lay on.

- **Lessons**
    1. Our values serve as our rules, beliefs, standards, and principles that guide how we live life and it largely affects where we choose to place our energy
- **Issues surrounding the subject matter**
    1. What are the contradictory values you hold that impede your capacity to practice antiracism?

_____
_____
_____
_____
_____
_____

- **Goals**
    1. To what length has your values aided your ability to exercise antiracism?

    _____
    _____
    _____
    _____
    _____

- **Action steps**
    1. Let go of the desire to be seen as a good person by others but explore what it looks like for you to hold white privilege and still uphold the practice of antiracism.
- **Checklist**
    1. Crosscheck that your core values and beliefs match your practice of lifelong antiracism.

DAY 27: YOU AND LOSING PRIVILEGE

YOU AND LOSING PRIVILEGE

The change will only come when we get rid of some of our white privileges. Did you just cringe? Well, it hurts to hear; but it is the hard truth. In life, you need to shed off some things for better and long-lasting gains. Here you need to let go of your privileges, comforts, and advantages as a white privilege holder just so that BIPOC's dignity is restored.

WHY DO YOU NEED TO LOOK AT LOSING PRIVILEGE?

Ways to lose some of your privileges for a greater good;

1. Talking to family and friends with white privilege about practicing antiracism.
2. Undergoing a personally sponsored antiracist education with available resources and not waiting for BIPOC to do that job for you.
3. Having an online or offline conversation on race with other white people.
4. Paying money and supporting more BIPOC businesses, projects, and entrepreneurial ventures.
5. Giving money to causes, organizations, and movements working towards freedom and dignity for BIPOC.
6. Intensifying the voices of BIPOC on whatever form of injustice.
7. Jeopardizing your comfort and relationships by speaking up instead of staying quiet.

- **Lessons**
    1. You need to let go of your privileges, comforts, and advantages as a white privilege holder just so that BIPOC's dignity is restored.
- **Issues surrounding the subject matter**
    1. Will you still agree to lose your white privilege haven learned all you have here?

    _____
    _____
    _____
    _____
    _____

    2. In what ways do you think your privileges ought to change in other to have full liberty to practice antiracism?

    _____
    _____
    _____
    _____
    _____

- **Goals**
    1. In what ways are you ready to let go of your white privileges just for the dignity of BIPOC?

    _____
    _____
    _____
    _____
    _____

2. What are the sets of comforts you are willing to use and how do you intend to go on without them?

_____
_____
_____
_____
_____

- **Action steps**
    1. You need to be willing to take risks and ready to make sacrifices.
- **Checklist**
    1. Harsh reality! For change to come, you need to lose some of your white privileges.

DAY 28: YOU AND YOUR COMMITMENTS (CONCLUSION)
YOU AND YOUR COMMITMENTS

By now a lot of emotions are running through you, but this is not the finish line of the antiracism race but the very beginning of a lifelong pursuit. Understanding the weight of white privilege and what it means to be personally complicit in the system of white supremacy is a lot to handle. Holding on to that load and that truth is very imperative in working with white privilege holders. Note every feeling you are experiencing now as it is part of the work. It is normal to feel the way you feel right now, without these feelings change will not occur because you cannot fix something until it is broken.

Allow the pain you feel break your heart open. Send out any attempt debarring from feeling this pain like color blindness, white Saviorism, and tokenism. It is this truth that gives your heart an opportunity for change. You have done a good job to be here so far, but we cannot let all we have learned go to waste. Uphold all the tenets of antiracism judiciously and committed to enabling the change you want to be seen. It doesn't end in promises, what will be done exactly to make sure this doesn't die away after today. I say this because it is in human nature to prefer what is comfortable, safe, and known; thus it is very easy to slide back to your former status quo but if you do the below, it will maintain your present momentum and deliver all you desire about antiracism. Here is some writing prompts you can use in crafting your commitment statements:

1. I am committed to challenging my white fragility …
2. I am committed to challenging racism in other people with white privilege …

3. I am committed to showing up for this lifelong antiracism work because…
4. I am committed to continuing my lifelong antiracism education …
5. I am committed to being a good ancestor …
6. I am committed to uplifting, supporting, and centering BIPOC by…
7. I am committed to challenging my optical allyship …
8. I am committed to continuing my lifelong antiracism education …
9. I am committed to breaking through my white apathy by…and many more.

Try to build on the above and write out your pledges as it related to the antiracism work. Pledges help to the main focus on the job at hand. Paste them boldly at home, work, or anywhere you will be able to see it every day and be reminded of your commitment. To be more accountable to your commitments, share your goals with someone who has a niche for social change and antiracism. Treat your commitment as a living and evolving phenomenon and your commitment will help your antiracism work become a lifelong practice.

- **Lessons**
    1. Antiracism is not hugely dependent on perfectionism but to help create change alongside consistent commitment, learning, showing up, and doing all necessary so that BIPOC can live with equality and dignity.
- **Issues surrounding the subject matter**

1. What are the significant changes you will make in life, people you need to call out/in, apologies ad announcements you need to make, and organizations/bodies you need to volunteer at to start your antiracism work?

   _____
   _____
   _____
   _____
   _____
   _____
   _____
   _____
   _____

- **Goals**

   1. How do you intend to stay committed from Day 29 forward and upholding the tenets of antiracism?

      _____
      _____
      _____
      _____
      _____

   2. Craft your commitments to help you uphold the tenets of antiracism and make sure to re-pledge this often.

      _____
      _____
      _____

_____

_____

- **Action steps**

    1. Make sure your commitments and actions are feasible enough in other to be held accountable for them.

- **Checklist**

    1. There is no clean and comfortable way to disassemble a violent system of oppression. Roll up your sleeves and get dirty, the work must be done.

The walls of white supremacy can crumble if we apply the right tools in carrying out that challenging task. But it starts with us first and then our community. BIPOC can live a life free of racism and oppression. Be an agent of positive change the world needs and be among the exceptional list of good ancestors.

Thanks

We Congratulate you for taking that ultimate decision

And buying this Workbook, we hope the reason for getting this workbook was achieved. We've tried our best to bring you this great workbook, but we're human and make mistakes. Please, if you notice any error whatsoever, you can write to us olavictichy@gmail.com and I'll do my best to Respond in Time.

However, You can Take out a little of your Time To Rate Us on Amazon.

Also we appreciate you for believing in Us and Buying this Workbook. May all Your Goals Actualize this Year!

Other Books By Same Author

CPSIA information can be obtained
at www.ICGtesting.com
Printed in the USA
LVHW080425230620
658711LV00019B/3336